A FLAME IN YOUR HEART

A FLAME IN YOUR HEART

Kathleen JAMIE   Andrew GREIG

BLOODAXE BOOKS

ISBN: 1 85224 017 2

First published 1986 by
Bloodaxe Books Ltd,
P.O. Box 1SN,
Newcastle upon Tyne NE99 1SN.

Bloodaxe Books Ltd acknowledges subsidy
from the Scottish Arts Council towards
the publication of this book.

Bloodaxe Books Ltd also acknowledges
the financial assistance of Northern Arts.

Typesetting by Bryan Williamson, Manchester.

Printed in Great Britain by
Tyneside Free Press Workshop Ltd, Newcastle upon Tyne.

Acknowledgements

We would like to thank Mrs Rita Jamieson of Hillhead, Orkney, and Mr Mark English of Manor Farm, Wateringbury for the use of 'Quoylobs' and Battle Street during the writing of this book. Also Mr Sean Kane at Trent University, Ontario for his critical guidance.

Among our source material, the following books were particularly important: Angus Calder's *The People's War* (Cape), Richard Hillary's *The Last Enemy* (Macmillan), Len Deighton's *Fighter* (Cape).

A shortened version of this book was broadcast by BBC Radio 4 in 1985 under the title *Rumours of Guns* (producer: Patrick Rayner).

Some of these poems have previously appeared in *New Edinburgh Review*, *The Scotsman*, *New Scottish Writing*, and in Kathleen Jamie's *Black Spiders* (Salamander Press, 1982).

The lines opposite are from the song 'I Don't Want to Set the World on Fire' by Marcue, Benjemin, Durham and Seiler. The quotation on page 77 is from 'In Memory of Eva Gore-Booth and Con Markiewicz' by W.B. Yeats.

The illustrations on pages 9 and 75 are by James Cramb. The front cover Spitfire photograph is reproduced by kind permission of the Imperial War Museum. The back cover photograph by Irene Reddish was taken at Beamish North of England Open Air Museum.

AG/KJ

'I don't want to set
The world on fire,
I just want to start
A flame in your heart.'

One by one they will return,
throttling down over perimeter wires
of remembered airfields, then taxi up
to abandoned huts.

They look around in the rain.
There are pigs in the Control Tower,
in a shelter one finds an old 'Picture Post',
a French letter between the pages.
They shrug and laugh, the youngest
bites his lip.

They share cigarettes, and talk
for an hour by the Dispersal Hut,
then one by one take off and climb
above the clouds, where it is always blue,
burning and burning at that summer's end.

I.

Then we heard the guns around Gravesend
as they hit the docks, broke off the match
to step outside and see the show.
'Why ain't you lads up there
knockin' 'em down?' Our searchlights
drained to nothing in the dark.
Al drawled 'Mom won't let Lennie fly at night
and me, I never did like overtime.'
I smiled to myself, though our flak
was just a gesture. 'Let's hope you shoot
better than you throw, mate' –
these boys were set on beating us
and with their home crowd looking on
it was friendly, but a bit of needle too.
We went inside, nothing we could do.

> Draughtsmanship has always been my line,
> not women. I smudge the dance-hall sketches.
> But maybe this time I've struck lucky . . .

I'm no darts player, never have been.
Better at deflection-shooting, no time
to hesitate, and Al our Prairies joker
is always on the wild side. The opposition,
two local lads, were frankly in a different class
but we'd had two pints while waiting
for the girls, hit a hot streak, were holding them.

> How light a girl is when you dance,
> how far removed from a machine!
> She's way out of my class: left University
> to nurse; better spoken, smart as paint,
> pretty as a – excuse me while I gibber!

A sparky girl. Her cool look is
the challenge I would rise to.
We made a date with her and friend (Al
did the talking and I the eager nods):
the 'Darnley Arms', Friday, twenty hundred hours
God and Goering willing . . .

They didn't show up. Who'd blame them.
It had been a speculative shot. We're
not officers, I'm no Clark Gable,
one look at Al shows what's on his mind
('I want to roll little Rosie
from here to Wisconsin . . .')
We agreed to one last decider, then leave.

They got away first throw but so did we,
rattled down great style from 501.
Then I'm standing with 50 to shoot,
three arrows in my hand, the local aces
needing only double tops. 'When the going
gets tough . . .' Al whispers. 'You can do it, eh?'
I put down my pipe, real casual like
and toed the line. Hit the 10, went for tops,
tensed up, hit the ruddy wall. Someone laughed,
I hesitated, and in that bright room felt alone,
not tough at all, and in the knowledge of defeat
drew my arm back anyway –

the street-door opened,
I glanced, turned back, threw –

the moment it left my hand I was sure.
No bombs, no war could change it now.
My dart slid through the smokey air, thud:
Double Twenty.

Hubbub, laughter, Al's cowboy whoop, mine host
set us up a pint apiece – 'Reckon these lads
did for you, George old son.' 'Reckon so'
said George, turning back to the board,
'won't be so lucky next time, though.'
We pushed over to our girls . . .

    She smiled, I smiled, there was
no flap, no hurry. Though she had class
I had my moments and that might do,
would blooming have to! 'What was all
the fuss about?' 'We got lucky
and won against the run of play.'
'I see . . .' she said, and took my arm
just like that, going through to the Snug.

And when she turned to me again
I seemed to see what she'd say next,
what I'd say, how it would all turn out,
as though a searchlight had just leapt
forward in the dark, and we had always known its mark.

Not what you'd imagine, not posh,
not Educated, bit silly, asks all the questions.
No moustache, more's the pity.
Not brave, I don't think. Said next to nothing
about flying (shame!) but left the glamour
to the loud-mouth yank (Canadian, actually)
who dribbled over Rosie. Not that
she cared, you know *her*. Anyhow

they threw about their money,
showed off, talked darts (I ask you!)
and histories. I suppose they can't
talk shop, we're trained Not to Get Involved –
so how do we Get Intimate? We didn't
want them to walk us home, you know,
said goodnight at the door
(doubt he'd ever kissed before!)

Shan't be long till he's posted
elsewhere. Sad really, he's sweet. (Confess:
said 'yes' to a date next week. Name's Len.)

I woke round 5.00, my head still swampy
with booze and fags – some carry-on!
Did we really make complete
asses of ourselves, did Al . . . ?

A glass of water in the dawn,
held to the half-light then glolloped down.
Another. 'For Christ's sake shut
the bloody door!' 'Appleton!'

Clear water through my muddy guts,
low bands of mist, unmoving tips
of poplars and dock cranes; in Parsonage Farm
a woman leading horses from the yard . . .

So I went for a run
across the common, down a lane,
up the ridgeway and into the trees,
leaping and dodging through nettles and

cowpats like squashed hats,
scattering rabbits, pheasants, squirrels,
arms and legs going like bilge-pumps
spilling my rotten carcase of slop,

pure June crashing through my lungs
as I chose at each fork
on impulse without delay or doubt,
in love with swerve and onrush –

Grabbed a cold shower, kitted up,
bolted breakfast ('Out wenching, son?'),
jumped on the truck as we shot down the lane
through the orchard, old Goosey driving . . .

Let it come!
I'm seeing her Thursday. No worries, no fear.
Alive till we die, that much is clear.
It's going to be a scorcher, you can tell.

The moment a kiss comes to an end,
we open our eyes, read consent in one another's
and kiss again, more forcefully,
we could be other lovers. Is it when
I'm mesmerised by the slow unwinding
bandage in my hand that you grow distant
from the pilots' room, feel us, dancing?
Till someone digs your ribs, exclaims
'Come on, mate, your deal!'
Sometimes we just step outside, as lovers will
for a breath of air, those narrow halls
where a dance-band's marking time.

The past blooms anywhere
I don't care. My roots
are in our future; everything
ah, *stems* from this.
I am a pirate with this rose
clenched between my teeth:
your lipstick kiss left on my lips . . .

Forgive me, I am light-
headed and everything's
a little upside-down today.
We're turning mellow
in the sun; nothing's doing,
the war's a phoney lark
ringing somewhere out of sight
that brings us here to tan
in deckchairs, and cultivate
our languid slang.

The sun's burnt off the dew
and cornfields shiver as they
inch towards harvest . . .
The same wind blows through me
from head to heart to heels.
I would be dancing, cheek
to cheek with this long summer.
That's how it feels,
my darling, this
is how it feels.

I rather think you're outside, too
in shirt-sleeves, watching
those early stars call in. Lord knows,
you could be up through all those angels,
sky beneath, knowing only twisted heat, this instant.

They say the source could be long blown out
by the time the light reports;
deadweight falling through the dark
to smash another star. Imagine:
I may be witnessing that final wink . . .

Car doors are slamming, they're
laughing at the bar.
Your letter came this morning, ages late.
It says 'I am', 'we are'.

Sunlight splitting white beams through trees like at the pictures
angled down from projector to forest-floor screen   I
walked right into it   clatter and flash
I jerked aside   (black and white crosses
sun in my eyes – two magpies)   hawthorn   hogweed   nettles
sharp reek in the whitebeam   each leaf

That's what it's like now   (if anyone asks)
on-screen not onlooking
alive like never before   moving
among gay heroes   lovely gals   bang bangs
sharp to the last leaf   last fingernail

Living in focus, some feeling.

Twenty angels below is scarcely an audience
makes no odds   it's what you do
when no one is looking   that counts
it comes clear   you stop acting   and act

We were carrying our dance shoes,
keeps them good, saves our corns.
Darkness, miles, and not so much as a match.
Rose yanked me into a ditch. Too late,
it glanced my leg. Huge car, soft and fast.
Never slowed at all. 'Near thing!' she says.
Neither light nor sound, could have been dreaming.
I was crying. Rose rubbed the dirt and bruises.
I stared into the blackout. They just purr on happily.
Stared again. Saw red. It dawned on me. The war, I mean.

II.

A summer seen through perspex, glaze
and the head turning, turning,
missing the little things, the specks that grow . . .

The wooden handle of a trowel
fallen among flowers, spent matches,
white knuckles, secateurs glinting
in a mottled hand, dead heads
flipped onto the grass . . .

'Someday in the future – ' Len began.
'The future!' laughed the Hon
Harold Algernon St John, 'What future?'
And examining the crossword in the 'Daily Mail',
'Six letters, a following shade *– any ideas, old man?'*

'Shadow?' Len replied.

I wanted excitement, a woman (admit it,
a lark), bored stiff on my arse at 'Stafford & Meeks'
drawing elevations of houses I'd never afford:
must be more, I thought, must be more.

Now I've gone and done it.

I never believed that it would be
so bloody, so intimate (and frequently dull).
Terrifying. Yet when you give yourself away
and get life back again, unexpectedly,
walking in the evening you will see
houses, trees, faces, all sharpened in intense relief.

What you said about being shot down –
I think I know (I shouldn't compare). At the bus stop
someone was reading the news. I strained
to see the list, you know, of names,
caught sight of what looked like 'Appleton'. The rain
came on, drops landing on the page
spread through. He folded it away
before I could see if it was true.

There was a sort of quiet feeling, as if
wardrobes and pianos were falling silently downstairs,
before the plummet, what happened you said
when you were hit, how the ground rears up like a rabid mare.
I couldn't stop falling down this spiral pit, expecting
to meet rock, or the sea. All the time I was changing sheets.
Jane was kind, though I didn't say. When she spoke,
it was like a wireless playing to an empty Mess.

It was four hours before I saw a paper. The name
was Applethwaite. Remember when you pushed
the stick into the hand of the blind man who'd
who'd dropped it, and was panicky? I felt like him,
like you lads when you regain control,
lift the aircraft out of its spin, get the earth
beneath again. Len, I can't help but imagine
this crumpled shape: your plane; *Mrs* Applethwaite.

A catch in the throat the tannoy's
click before it blares –
he's on his way.

Pencil rolls to the edge, flips . . .

A ring of moisture on his seat,
the pencil rattling on the floor,
irritation at that broken tip
as he runs into the glare –

between the power coming on
and the details of command,
a lucid interval, a break
from narrative.

May you go your rounds
in peace so far as possible
among the complaints and silences,
the politeness of the dying
and the moody convalescent
chewing over the sour grapes
his friends have left.
May even Matron smile, God rot her,
when this letter comes through
and let you read it sitting on
an unmade bed, curls escaping
your cap to swing at the nape
of your neck and wring
a smile from the 'improving'
and bring no bitterness to those
who are beyond sex, wanting
only mother –

I know it is the in-between
who break your heart, those
who will live but never be whole.
Your anger feels like stitches being torn.
You'll fold this away, work on.
There is no mending it.

She scans the same horizon
from the other side
and I can almost touch her hands,
her kiss falls just too light.

Fraulein, one of us will burn tonight.
The other will waltz with an airman,
listen to the day's war news.
And I can almost reach her hands.

The machine
the machine is in the sky
the machine in the sky is burning and falling

Inside the machine a burning uniform
inside the uniform a burning man
inside the man a small boy

fighting to take control
of all the screaming
that surrounds him

Dear Katie,

Had a bit of a shakey-do yesterday, but no flap, I'm fine. We busted up a swarm of bombers over Deal, went in line-astern, real copybook stuff (they want to throw that book away, like many things it's gone out of date fast). Tallyho bambambam etcetera. Hellofa-goodshow – Brian T. got 2 then baled out, Al and Hughie 1 each, I added a probable. Then the 109s bounced us, total shambles all round it happens so bloody fast chaps squalling on the headphones hot metal breakfasts whizzing about trying to survive the next few seconds that's all . . . I'm sorry to say Don's had it, and one of our new blokes, can't remember his name. Then I spotted Tim with one of the bastards ('scuse) on his tail roughing him up, so went down to put my oar in – got him, I think – stopped looking behind and one of the other side must have gone down to look after *his* mate because he nailed me good and proper, starboard wing folds up and a bonfire at my ankles and my kite is definitely on the way down and out, trouble is she wanted to take me with her, cockpit hood jammed and things got a bit hot and bothered – bloody frighten-ing, actually – till I sort of fell out and floated down to Merrie England minus a shoe but the foot's still there so I ain't complaining! I landed smack in a plum orchard so I'm dangling up in this tree with half a dozen giggling Land Girls trying to decide what to do about it when this wrinkly old geezer comes along and shouts up 'Just dropped in for a cuppa, then?' and nearly ends himself laughing . . . Failed to come up with devastating reply, so confined myself to a simple gesture.

So that was that. I'm all right, really. A bit like your toast – a little burned, a little scraped, but sound enough under all that. Tim's a bit shot up but he'll pull through. The good news is I've a week's leave till I'm fully operational again (they want to keep me from writing off more expensive machinery) and I've an Immodest Prop-osal: would you care to spend a couple of days at a little pub I came across down Wateringbury way? Can you? No strings attached. You know. Tim's loaned me his old banger and petrol coupons, not a bad bloke for an officer. It would be good to see you and spend more than a few hours together – sun, cider, sweet nothings. Can do? Love as ever,

Len

P.S. Like the typing? Hand temporarily SNAFU.

xx

Darling Len,

And the good news is – Can do! I've two days off, now it's Nights and Splits till Doomsday, still, small beer compared to *you*, O hero! You'll need your favourite nurse to hold your hand, the good one, that is. And a CAR! Oh, I hear the hiss of snakes from the corridor: the Gorgon's coming. Must look busy. And I must know more! Till then, don't drink, TAKE REST, you'll pick me up? Forgive me if I gush . . .

with love

We would not draw curtains
over the sharp little panes, we
liked to keep the old rooms fresh,
to smell woodsmoke, leaves,
and hear the cock in the morning.

At night I could watch
constellations rise and call
for his attention; his response
made me forget their names,
rattled the frames a while.

'Finest summer I remember' Old George says
without irony, straightening his hollyhocks.
Right enough, the sun day after day
and nowhere to hide in the sky, men charred
to wavering black sticks against the glare,
then soft thuds in the night, fruit-fall
and bruised lovers giggling in the lanes . . .

Wasps crawled from the plums she picked
but were too groggy to fly or sting
and I felt drugged with heavy juice,
leaning to flick them from her arm . . .

'Keep out of mischief' Old George leers
and hee-haws as he shuffles off, leaving me
fingers clenched round a windfall Cox's
still fizzling at the edge of my last bite –
I sling it away and hurry to find her
before heat goes out of the day.

He is 25, it is the last day
of his leave, and my whole world
rests gently against him. His arm
will tingle when he wakes! Keep peace,
keep still as the wallpaper birds
while the living take up their songs.
I feel the dawn of tenderness
I haven't known before. He's mine,
who can doubt it now morning shines
on us, on this aged mattress?
But the blue birds are painted forever
unmoved. We're young,
it's the last day of his leave. Wake him!

Shaken awake in the dark,
mug of tea, sign the chit,
wool, sheepskin, leather, pull on
animal layers, feel mechanical,
wet grass, cold metal, world grey
as me, entering the machine –

As we climb I think of you sleeping.
What use is thought? It can't touch.
5.00 a.m., the hour the ghosts give up.
Cold up here, glazed, nothing doing,
patrolling the coast at 18,000 . . .
How come the sun keeps rising through slaughter?
Goes to show we're not much, just as well.
If the world were batted round by us
it would bounce like a ping-pong ball
between Heaven and Hell, till it was
cracked as we are –

We've been looking and looking but
met with nothing but light, and now
throttle down over familiar trees,
thinking of bacon as the appetite awakes.
Touching down, the earth
reaches up and murmurs beneath me
like you when I returned to bed.
I feel myself lit up, confirmed,
as I slide from the cockpit to the ground.

We don't have seasons, we just repeat
the same on a groaning train of men
who get discharged at the other end.
Under our hands, nothing changes.

I want to be a Land Girl with itching eyes,
I want you to see me rise from a wheat field,
stretch to ease an aching back, drive tractors
through orchards, let the sun slap me, sweat,
let the grime smeared on my brow run into furrows
that will turn into wrinkles one day. Not yet.
Let us girls throw our arms around each others' necks,
smell cattle and soil, give that direct
feminine leer to trucks passing full
of lewd soldiers. Let me cut down a harvest.
I want to take tea-breaks lying flat on my back,
to accept without question whatever pictures occur
in the clouds. Just let me get these
damned stockings off. I'd walk home at twilight,
cry with the cows if I wanted,
instead of holding it back like a show of bad temper.

Out in the fields is death at its best:
owls pick off the slowest mice, moles'
skin-and-bone dangle from fences. I want
growth: dirt on my delicate hands.

'FIRST forget the jousting,
the "chivalry of the air" guff.
All that went out with France.
The meek inherit the earth all right,
six feet down in bloody no time.

SECOND no mixing it
with the Abbéville kids.
We hit the bombers, 109s are out.
Not magnificent, but it's war.

THIRD ambush, not duelling.
Whenever possible we go in
with sun and height on our side.
Pick the straggler, get in close,
nail him, get the hell out.
And forget the fancy acrobatics,
those tight formations that went down well
with the brass hats and ladies.
The Display days are over.

FOURTH the WAAFs on this base
are strictly off-limits
and that's official: paws off!

FIFTH stay alive.
Drink if you must,
sleep when you can.
Get through the first week
and you're in with a chance.

SIXTH this round is on me.
What'll yours be? Double Scotch?'

Some bloody pep-talk, eh? 'Scuse language.
It's the same whenever new boys arrive
(and they come and go quite fast now).
But the CO's right, dammit, method
is part of our madness.
Just never let me catch
me making love to you like that.

You'd think the simple pale blue page
a window, so clearly can I see through
to the Dispersal Hut. They were
fully kitted up. It's hot, they sweat,
Canadian Al plays cat's cradle, hums,
two kip in chairs, there's
the occasional flick of a page
of 'Picture Post'. And Len, the one
who must keep busy, his
left hand's thrust knuckle deep in his hair.
He leans over the table, puts the date,
locks his ankles, writes 'Dear Katie',
and tells his news. Always in pencil –
the schoolboy, the apprentice
in his 'hell of a fellow' flying kit.
How the point wears down to dull
and flat, at the foot of the page,
where he says 'We've flown four sorties already today'.

I went to visit Tim last night. He's a
little pale, but what do you expect.
He says thanks for the cigs and wants to book
'a slow smoochie with the poppet',
that is, a dance with you.
Says he'll be a little stiff but maybe
you could help with that. Winked. Swine!
I said I'm fighting to protect my girl
from hogs like you. 'Any excuse, old boy,
any excuse will do' – then an inward smile
quite at odds with his posh drawl
and that preposterous moustache . . .

We stood at the window in the dark,
sharing a cigarette as the bombers went over.
His hand shook on his stick, I helped him
to a chair. His hip is worse
than I'd realised, he'll not fly again.
'Well out of it' I said. Silence.
I'm a fool. You understand
I love the man. The far-off thud
of Bofors guns – shooting in the dark but
you have to put up some kind of a show.
He shook his head, lit up another,
never said a word.

I left with the All Clear, got a lift
from our Adjutant, he'd been visiting his son.
We didn't talk much. The night was clear,
there were many stars. I thought:
not all the faint ones are far away,
nor all the bright ones near,
some fuzzy things are galaxies.
It seemed important, I hung on to it
as the bitter smoke of Woodbine stung my eyes.

'Bloke next to Eddie died in the night,'
the Adj. said. 'Spare a fag?'
We hit something on the road.
'What was that?' 'Dunno, something small.'
We didn't stop. 'Well out of it, I reckon.'

I shook my head, lit up for two, passed one over.

III.

He was mine, no doubt about it.
A lumbering Stuka, too low to dive,
too slow to run – I checked my tail
and went in.
                My first burst
shattered his canopy, the second
blew his head off.
I was very close.
The slipstream caught the neck,
the stub of the neck,
and as the blood kept pumping out
smeared it back along the fuselage
in ragged streams – like raindrops
across the windows of a train –
bright red on grey, right back
to the tail, then flecked
across the cross.
                It flew on
for a full 30 seconds, then
entered the sea.
I thought: the plane's so stable
why have pilots at all? In the future
we will not be necessary.
Then I turned, flew home for lunch.
No. 4. I am one helluva fellow.

What have I done?

Nothing.

If you knew that little force
when I press stamps, then unthinking
watch my letter fall into the box . . .

That gentle touch
I feel beneath my ears
as you raise my face to yours . . .

I still kiss you, though I know
that soft pressing of the thumb
is all it takes to kill a man.

. . . into the shelter here come the planes
they are silver and have no wings
they drop their load nothing explodes
a sound like footballs bouncing
I look out the strip is thick
with severed heads

one rolls at my feet it is
for me personally I lift it up
the hair grips my fingers so I
cannot put it down I
am going to recognise this
the face swings round
                              we dive . . .

You know they stick patches
across the muzzles of our guns
each time the plane's re-armed –
renewable virginity we blast away
each time we enter the dark embrace
that makes us serious, that lets us laugh
so willingly; it's in our eyes.

The armourers mutter
when we return unbroken; I'd say
they're checking up on us to see
we've been with the bad lads again.
I've known fellows fire off
at empty air rather than suffer
the sidelong glance and knowing grin.

They'd make us innocent again
but it's not on, nor would I want
this knowledge undone or concealed.
I want to know you again and again
and trail my fingers round your mouth;
I fall asleep dreaming of cannons
and metal peeling back like skin –

you will not muzzle me when I cry out.

The moon has set. At last
the ducks I watched asleep
at the edges of their pond,
fat and warm, are stirring.
You ought to know: I'm very late,

and sway between a silly pride,
a need: to grow large and round
as if by magic, as if I knew
I contained the world
and was besotted. Then fear:

I hold my head. My world will split,
the two halves fall and
gently rock, like cradles.
I waken early, listen for my familiar
ache. Should you wonder,

that is, not want to know,
count me among your 'possibles'.
We'll go to London. Blend
with the other widows there, real
or feigned. I shan't use your name.

I shan't even send this letter.
Not until I know. This, somehow, is my show.

Debriefed, giggling with adrenalin,
three men claim a kill apiece, each
babbling his account, nodding, compelling
gestures of the hands to show
how it was done ('250 yards – 2 second burst –
smoke, flames – a definite!') then seals
assertion with a cigarette.

But only one wreck is found.
They cannot believe it. They saw it all,
they were there! In the bar the action
is replayed, confirmed, each telling
more pure, more organised . . .

If truth were certified by sincerity and sweat!
The war goes on, nothing does much good
but a refusal to be fooled.

She counts the wrecks, observing silences.

He leans over his beer, elbows on knees,
I must say his name three times
before he answers. His arms are tanned,
the muscles move like light on water
as he takes his glass. Though he barely sips,
puts it down. He's tired.

Too tired to sleep. Even lets me unfasten
his jacket, mumbles about it scratching.
He breathes better without. But
I've seen him start awake

still trying to laugh. When it was a lark
he waited, one foot on the stile,
with his mocking look (you run funny!). Now
we meet like tyre on tarmac, one brief kiss,
his nerve

one more thing we don't discuss. Mum writes
about the evacuees getting healthy, looking
under strawberry leaves for fairies.
Not even wars halt seasons. But he doesn't
listen to the good things, even.

It's second nature now,
evasive action when someone tries
to get behind us. Close in and ask –
we'll laugh or blush or slip away.

We simply don't know how to stop,
still weaving as we lounge
with colleagues, friends, or pound
pissed and roaring at the bar.

Looking too long into her eyes
terrifies me. I sweat, mistake
fear for passion, and so lift roses
from a suburban garden, offer them

in a classy gesture –
She smiles, but isn't taken in.
Now she's turning inside me, closing
as I side-slip one more time –

I watch my tracers arc and seed
buds on the Hèinkel's fuselage
and sheer off only when they rush to bloom
into one monstrous rose –
Death's gardener, that's me.
Good at it, too. The hands that touch you
turn green in the glow of instruments,
itching for employment in His estate . . .
Katie, as I write this I'm picturing
myself kneeling as I push peas
into mild earth with my forefinger,
somewhere in Hampshire, early March,
light rain falling . . . We will marry, won't we,
for whenever I see you now I feel
the urge to plant, deep and patiently.
Are you shocked or smiling? I can't tell.
But if I live, something must grow –
children, sweet peas, the dreaming marrow's
long ear pressed to the ground –
to screen off that mushrooming bloom.

(Only nothing will make it go away now.
Marry, yes, but if we're going to burn,
we'll burn. Garden of a lifetime
flowered and withered in a flash . . .)

Have your garden. I'd like to see
the trees mature, and sit out there
till it's time to fold away the creaky chairs.
I want to live surrounded by the celery
and leeks you tend, the sleeves
rolled up your freckled arms.

Before the war I loved the bees.
Should I drowse in summer again,
I'd drift back here, and know the drone
as 'ours' or 'theirs', hear it chased
by Bofors guns, and jerk awake.
To be able to laugh! Only bees,
you knocking out an empty pipe.

IV.

Katie, the trees outside the boundary fence
have lost their leaves like old delusions
and it all looks rather dismal. That's
the lazy way to see it.
My training insists, with due respect
to poets, trees are not emotional
and stand for nothing –
which these do nicely. Their roots are deep
and when it really blows round here
they scarcely sway at all.

The sap is dropping down to safety
like our aircrew when the 'drome is strafed.
(Three times last week, now they're
refusing to come out. Scoundrels! Bloody right.)
We've withdrawn too, won't speak our thoughts,
becoming so polite of late, not wanting
our last words with someone to be rude –
uncertainty has made us trivial, not more true.

       *

Cameraderie? Within limits. There's still
Officers and Men (could we have a war
without such distinctions?)
Other day, Billy and me popped over
to Hornchurch, to pick up Mk. IIs.
Their Mess had been flattened and they
couldn't have me eat in the Officers'
so they suggest Billy eats inside while I
swill at a table outside the door.
There was nothing left to do
but spit on their food and leave –
so we did.
Good bloke, Billy, for a University type,
laughed like a drain all the way home.
Got a rocket of course, but they're
not going to ground us, so stuff 'em.

       *

When I walked back through the woods yesterday
there were whirrings and rustlings and I thought
animals run from us not out of fear
but because we embarrass them.
I met a man with a shotgun
and while we chatted it hung
from the crook of his arm, pointing
at my foot, and I wondered what he'd do
if I asked him to shoot.

Now the earth has stopped rising
and falling   he is carrying her
from the rubble   she has a print dress
pale hair   she could be
the child no one has   he
is weeping with gratitude she's
still alive   he hasn't yet seen
the dark cave pressed
pressed into one side of her head

I stand in the empty Mess, the bar is closed
but I've a half-bottle in my hand.
                    A wingman. Everyone should have one,
                    a guardian angel, a right hand man.
I look at the piano. ('Take the left hand, Lennie,
give me the fancy bits. Jeez don't they teach
you guys to boogie-woogie? Loosen up, eh . . .')
                    A light partner to my dark,
                    regardless is the word we use.
I lift the lid. Who would hear me
fingering the black notes at two in the morning?
                    I have hugged my life too close,
                    been full of death, Al, full of it.
I pour the spirit over the keys.
I take out my lighter.
                    Now I must be leader and wingman,
                    the victor rising and the victim going down.
The flame is steady in my unsteady hand.

Blood? Only port wine, suddenly drunk,
who's that giggling? Coughing on dust,
a stairway pointing up to the sky
naked and rude, terribly funny.

And a sharp tearing. I'm swearing,
there's fizzing and gurgling from severed
pipes, cuts on my legs, all the bells ringing
my head, here come people. Dust settles down
like a sigh. It all becomes clear.

Sharp as blades.
'I've torn my dress!' Laughing again.
The old barman who was chatting me up,
he's weeping over a stone. I mutter
'come now' so arch 'there's a war on, you know',

digging like a dog for a bone. Blue
to the lips, and I hear the word
he's about to utter, plea and command:
'Nurse?' Saw an arm. I thought:
'That's the last time I talk to strangers
in pubs. Should say I'm a typist.'

maybe she didn't die

          honestly   I walked away

all the others came running

          as much future follows from that

I didn't save her

          as would had I stayed

               (not for her not

Despise me? I shudder at 'murder'

          some kid over the river might

          tell her grandchild how the shockwaves

          rattled the windows

I have not cold eyes

          there I am fiddling with an eternity ring

          telling my son about 'during the war'

Forgive? (Ask a fighter
forgiveness

          the actions we don't

          just as effective

for not saving a life?

          how aware we become

          of dead friends, at parties.

    it's getting easier talking to you.

You'll never read this so here's the truth.

I'm getting drunk in a lousy pub in lousy London
and no lousy person talks to me thank God
except two tarts I can't afford on Flight Sergeant's pay.
Girls it's wine or women and tonight
it's wine to make me mindless though
as a matter of fact I ordered mild and got
bitter but that's the war for you . . .

They didn't take offence none intended and now
are getting giggly over port-and-lemon.
Why not? The bombs aren't near us tonight so
no flap it's everyone for themselves yet
what are we defending if not
some kind of human sympathy –
we've become madmen and machines to fight
madmen in machines, this is not temporary I think . . .

If I had money for these popsies I'd choose
the one who looks like you, ain't that romantic.
Go away girls, we can't afford
to throw ourselves away like this. A lift?
If we're all going West it might as well
be together. Painless, painless!
Pour me your taxi and take me home.
Hell none of us are beauties anymore.

V.

The daylight raids, the sun not setting
West, but East, a glare over Putney.
Punch drunk, we stagger in orbit,
and we don't know over whose roof-top
tonight it'll fall, red sky and warning.
We get up in the mornings, wondering why.
Reasons come, with the unpredictable risings,
the heat surprising our shoulders we expect from the East.

Lord I am old
or is it just there's no forgiveness.
I'm veteran at 24, antique
and scarred by careless handling;
   one foot shorter than the other,
   one arm awry – I feel
like a chair I want to rest forever in.
All I want is to be
   left out in the sun all day,
   brought in again at night.
Is there no restoring
   the injuries you do, and are
   done unto you.

*

I wash my face carefully each morning
with the hottest water I can find,
peer earnestly in the mirror –
   the lines won't wash off
   and you could pack
everything you need
for a month in the country
in the bags beneath his eyes.

*

   I never thought
   to live so long.
When we met that didn't matter.
That's the trouble with women,
   you let us come
   to want a future.
I never began to fear
   (scared stiff, yes)
till I began to hope for this.

*

Lord take me to the river.
Let her hands wash me down.
Forgiveness must wash over us
    equally, as the sunshine
    filled in the craters round our eyes
when we lay on the bank, fingers touching.
That touch is our only excuse
as the sun goes down to rumours of guns.

Walking home to mother's,
the church one` side of the river
on the other: the village.
And I'm laughing, pointing
to no one that the bridge
you must cross to the graveyard
and the country beyond
had been bombed. Gone,
but for the supports inclined
toward one another
and the river coursing through stones.

Billy – shell splinter nicked his optic nerve –
baled out blind from 20,000, fell through conflict,
felt his chute jerk, started counting down,
heard the earth ascend in order (lark,
dog barking, voices, *trees*, braced for impact –
a ploughed field).
He lay there bawling 'Stardust' till they found him.

'That earth under my arse felt good!
A gift. Somehow more than I deserved.
Blind,' he said carefully, facing the window,
'isn't a blackout, not like you'd think.
It's milky blue and makes the world more certain.'
Grinning, 'It's the last months were a blur.'

    I sat there sweating, couldn't speak.
    A lark was fizzling in the air outside . . .

'And Len,' frowning as he rolled a cigarette,
'half of them are mad, you know.
And most the rest, oh brave enough,
but numb or dumb, then die not knowing . . .
Work it out *now*, Lennie, there mightn't be
much time.' He lit up, smiled in my direction.
'And now I've shocked you.'

    I watched the shadow-branches
    close and open on the far blue wall,
    felt them part inside my chest . . .

'Easy to speak from the sidelines!
Just being alive is being in love,
don't you know that yet? It's a gift,
don't hug it . . . Anyway, how's Kate,
and are you taking that commission?'
'No.' My hand on his arm. 'Gotta go now . . .'

I left him then. No anger, no pity,
my God no fear. Blind isn't as imagined
and dead is not lying awake in the dark.
I know, I know. Set free,
like when a feverish child finally sees
the monster is a dressing-gown
then puts it on,
I walked out the final set of doors,
clear-headed, resolved, into the difficult light.

Say it straight, then:

Planes will be torched, but not this plane.
Men will be killed, but not this man.
Loves will sour, but not this love.

Here's the rumour
that keeps us going to the end.
Pass it on, pass it on . . .

*

Think clearly now, there is no other time.

Are we not men and women
who dress up and are deceived?

Why should we prove exceptions when
the rule's made up of those
who thought they were?

*

My hand on her breathing ribs. The fragility.

There is darkness everywhere
outside the circle of our lamp.
I'm lucid and awake, it's the middle
of the night and the only thing I felt
this hour before was dread. But
there are no monsters any more,
we've outgrown them, the space they left
is full again – of something else, not fear.
I used to hear them whispering if I'd done
something wrong. They've quite gone.
What woke me then? The moon can't penetrate
the blackout blinds; Len's sound:
dreaming of maps and aerodromes, and
keeping his options closed.
Except this one. Should I wake and tell him?
See him overawed, and wondering
'is it right?' It is. I know.

You never see them coming
two stray shells one entering the groin
one spraying the gut

  it is not as bad as you had imagined
  it is no worse than being born
  it is nearly over when you grasp it's begun

fumbling with suddenly yards of
slippery tubing spilling over the controls
tangled with oxygen and R/T leads
gauges clocks dials all connections coming undone
cords cut mind opening with the bowels
split jacket spreading behind you like
wings as you fall

  she may have stumbled and steadied herself
  between one bed and the next
  one hand grabbing a bedrail
  the other over her belly
  sweat along her hairline

in three seconds it's blurry almost comfortable
the hands wave vaguely
the mouth opens

ha –

        Len entering the fire he became.

War Widow

You know I keep the photograph
beside my bed. It gathers glances
like I could
when I swayed my way amongst airmen.

The trees behind you are still
fresh, your face never changes.

My stocking seams aren't quite so straight.
My uniform's returned. You wear yours
somewhere,
caught in a snapshot while you slept.

In an airless living-room in the new estate,
grouped round the feature fireplace,
they wait at readiness, looking up,
hands in pockets, wind ruffling their hair;
or hurrying past the breakfast-bar
in Mae Wests, eyes screwed against the sun,
nervy, slightly mad, done in.
One whistles 'Stardust' in the bath,
another stumbles dead-drunk in the hall,
his tan boots sunk a foot below the floor.
And the other one, the tired one who stands,
his long back turned, whose right arm hangs
crooked, always starting to turn round,
never fully turning round, who
speaks in the dark –

    We heard the guns around Gravesend
    as they hit the docks, broke off the match
    to step outside and see the show . . .

Above my bed the Airfix kits,
the Hurricane, Spitfire, Messerschmitt,
spun on their threads in the draught.

SPECIFICATION AND EVALUATION

AIRCRAFT: Supermarine Spitfire Mk.1

DESIGNER: Reginald Mitchell

MANUFACTURER: Vickers-Armstrong Ltd

TYPE: Fighter

YEAR: 1939

ENGINE: Rolls-Royce Merlin II, 12-cylinder V, liquid-cooled, 1030 hp

WINGSPAN: 36ft 10ins

LENGTH: 29ft 11ins

WEIGHT: 5,332 lbs

MAX SPEED: 355mph at 19,000 ft

CEILING: 34,000 ft

RANGE: 500 miles

ARMAMENT: 8 Browning machine guns (Calibre .303in, rate of fire 1,200 rds/min, supply carried 300 rds)

CREW: 1

AIRCRAFT: Hawker Hurricane Mk.1

DESIGNER: Sidney Camm

MANUFACTURER: Hawker Aircraft Ltd

TYPE: Fighter

YEAR: 1937

ENGINE: Rolls-Royce Merlin II, 12-cylinder V, liquid-cooled, 1030 hp

WINGSPAN: 40ft

LENGTH: 31ft 4ins

WEIGHT: 6,218 lbs

MAX SPEED: 322mph at 20,000 ft

CEILING: 33,400 ft

RANGE: 525 miles

ARMAMENT: 8 Browning machine guns (Calibre .303in, rate of fire 1,200 rds/min, supply carried 300 rds)

CREW: 1

'Both beautiful, one a gazelle'

Andrew Greig is a mountaineer and freelance writer. *Kingdoms of Experience*, his account of the 1985 assault on the unclimbed North-East Ridge of Everest has just been published by Hutchinson. *Summit Fever* (Hutchinson, 1985), his book about the 1984 British Mustagh Tower expedition in the Karakoram Himalayas, was runner-up for the Boardman Tasker Award for Mountaineering Literature. In 1986 he climbed with the British Lhotse Shar expedition.

He has published three books of poems: *White Boats* (Garret Arts, 1972), *Men On Ice* (Canongate, 1977), and *Surviving Passages* (Canongate, 1982). He won an Eric Gregory Award in 1973, and received a Scottish Arts Council Writer's Bursary in 1975, and again in 1985. He was writer in residence at Glasgow University in 1979-81 and Scottish/Canadian Exchange Fellow in 1982-83.

He was born in 1951 in Bannockburn, Stirlingshire. After studying Philosophy at Edinburgh University, he worked as a salmon fisherman, advertising copywriter and farm labourer. He now lives in Anstruther, Fife.

Kathleen Jamie won a Gregory Award at 19, which enabled her to travel in the Near East, and later to the Himalayas. She won a Scottish Arts Council Book Award for her first collection, *Black Spiders* (Salamander Press, 1982), and in 1985 received a Scottish Arts Council Writer's Bursary.

At 24 she is the most outstanding young woman poet now writing in Britain. Her first full-length book of poems, *The way we live*, will be published by Bloodaxe in 1987.

She was born in 1962 in Renfrewshire, studied Philosophy at Edinburgh University, and has made a living from odd jobs such as archaeological "digger" and Pizza Hut waitress. She is now a freelance writer, and lives in Edinburgh with two tyrannical cats and a mountaineer.